CW00672223

4
PILLARS OF
ABUNDANT LIFE

ASHOK WAHI

PARTRIDGE

ISBN: Hardcover 978-1-5437-0735-9
      Softcover 978-1-5437-0734-2
      eBook   978-1-5437-0736-6

Print information available on the last page.

To order additional copies of this book, contact
Partridge India
000 800 919 0634 (Call Free)
+91 000 80091 90634 (Outside India)
orders.india@partridgepublishing.com

www.partridgepublishing.com/india

Paramahansa Yogananda
(January 5, 1893 — March 7, 1952)
Picture courtesy: Self Realization Fellowship

The book is a humble offering to Paramahansa Yogananda, my blessed and worshipful guru, for his eternal love and divine teachings!

Lord Ganesha. Painting by Anita

In loving memory of my parents and my wife, Anita.

Anita and my mother, were two of the most loving and caring persons I have ever known!

My father's love of good books, good life, and high moral values; and my mother's devotional nature and love, have shaped and influenced my entire life.

CONTENTS

TESTIMONIALS

It has been my good fortune to know Ashok for almost three decades. When he came into my life as my manager in my professional career in the 1990s, who would have guessed that he would continue to guide me as my 'manager' through this life journey! Ashok has always been there to provide guidance, advice and support as I tread this life path. He has given me clarity and direction, in times, when my own understanding was muddied.

—Srikant Srinivasan, Head – Services, GE Healthcare South Asia

To sum up my relationship with Mr. Wahi in a single sentence; he is my FPG - Friend, Philosopher, Guide.

I have known him for more than a decade but we had lost touch over time. When I met him again at the time of starting my own business, it was like Godsend. He was just the friend I needed at that time in life. From that moment on, I always

go to him with my fears, sorrows, and anxieties. And even without my telling him much, he always knows what to say to soothe my aching heart and soul. He gives selflessly and is always there when you need him.

I am able to unravel my thoughts and take the right decision within a single conversation with him. I feel blessed to have someone with such vast wisdom as my friend and go to person.

—Meenal Sinha, Founder CEO,
Meetings and Offices, Mumbai

I have had the pleasure and privilege to know Ashok for two decades; first as a colleague and friend, and later as a mentor. My interactions with Ashok has been a transformative experience as our conversations are always focused on him asking just the right questions to force me to think in ways I have not considered before. I have seen myself grow in new ways, past preconceived notions of my limitations and my own self.

—Sanjai K, Partner,
E&Y Consulting, Bangalore

I had met Ashok a decade back, in a stressful and noisy project environment where he was an exception! He is a person filled with love, positivity and humbleness, with no traces of ego in him.

He also introduced me to spirituality and his guru, Paramahansa Yogananda, which gave a new direction to my life. Much later in life I realized that the behavior of a true devotee is a reflection of his guru, and it is so true for Ashok!

Sir, thank you for being an honest friend, guide and a teacher. Stay blessed and write many more books!

—Abhinav Tiwari, Regional Director, Capgemini Consulting, Singapore

True to his name, Ashok is some one who is beyond the temporal world of desires, frustrations and the consequent sorrow! My journey with him dates back to 1982 when even as a sprightly young man, he had a different world vision.

38 years later, I hail him as my spiritual guru, who, through his little messages often unreciprocated

by me, has given the much-needed daily knock at my heart's door. Almost supernaturally, his most apt communications and writings have come at the most significant junctures, helping me resolve many a conflict and dilemma! He understands the unsaid, addresses the core, and stimulates me to find my own inner space! I see the spiritual connect; the guidance our Creator sends to the lesser mortals like me, through people like Ashok.

May the '4 Pillars of Abundant Life' fortify the weak, heal the bruised, ignite hope in the hearts of the frustrated, weary ones, and bring an everlasting smile of contentment and serenity, the twin-rewards of any spiritual journey!

—Sangeeta Hajela, Principal, Delhi Public School, Indirapuram, Delhi

After my divorce, I was jobless, trapped in a society that questioned my self-worth. While everyone saw me for my mistakes - Mamu, Mr. Ashok Wahi, saw me for what I was: a human being.

He taught me how to lead a balanced, abundant life through reading, meditation, and healthy

lifestyle. Most important of all, he helped me rebuild my confidence to chase my dreams. Today, I am happily remarried in a healthy relationship, living and working abroad in Brazil, and pursuing my master's degree from an American university.

Whatever I am today is thanks to his benevolent guidance and love.

—Hansa Narang Gohl, Teacher,
Curitiba, Brazil

I have been blessed to experience unconditional love and endless support from this "human angel", whom I met four years back. Ashok uncle treated me as his own daughter, supporting my overseas education when the bank refused a loan. He taught me fearlessness, generosity and service through his actions. His attitude towards life and way of recognizing the flow of energy in the physical world is magnificent. He continues to be the positive guiding light in my life despite the massive distance.

—Uma Patwardhan, Teacher,
Queensland, Australia

Ashok has been a friend and guide for more than 30 years to me. He has steered my life with his positive thoughts, messages and spiritual guidance during the most challenging times, providing a perspective that is so realistic.

The year 2020 was the most difficult as I struggled through depression, heart condition, and cancer amidst the pandemic. One of the most important things that kept me going were the messages from Ashok in the morning, especially when it was difficult to get up from bed. Ashok became my go to person for understanding what was happening. He helped me at each step and his words: that it was all 'maya, an illusion,' gave me the much needed, potent and deeper perspective. This was most helpful to me.

I am a regular reader of his Blog too, which is filled with wisdom.

It is a blessing to have you Ashok, as a friend, philosopher and guide in our lives.

—Dr. Jyotiee Mehraa,
Ex Program Manager UNODC

Throughout the past three decades that I have known Ashok uncle, he has generously shared his wisdom with me, and hundreds of people around the world who follow his advice on growing spiritually and living happily.

Ashok uncle's life story is instructive. An introspective, deeply passionate, evolved engineer certainly has something to teach us all. As a first-principles thinker with no fear of speaking his truth, Ashok uncle's thoughts are often unique and thought provoking. His instinct for seeing through life's veneer has changed how I see the world.

I've learned an enormous amount from Ashok Uncle. Reading, listening, and applying his principles of spiritual growth and happiness has given me calm confidence on my path and taught me to enjoy every moment of this journey. Closely studying his actions has shown me how great things are accomplished through small, persistent steps, and how large an impact one individual can have.

—**Pallavi Nadella**, Sr. Program Manager, Apex Supply Chain Technologies, Mason City, USA

His words are simple and yet profound. And his words and stories touch a chord with everyone who reads them regardless of age, culture or background.

I am grateful to have him in my life as a pillar of love, and aspire to embrace each day as he does, with courage, humility, a sense of abundance, and overflowing joy.

—Chaitanya Jayanti, Manager, Northwestern Medicine, Chicago, USA

I was fortunate to have met and befriend this enlightened soul during one of our group meditations. Since then I have received so much guidance from Ashokji on leading a balanced, peaceful and joyous life. In fact he's a living example of the ideal life most of us merely wish to live! Just listening to his experiences and how he dealt with situations, is a powerful guide to dealing with my own.

The most crucial counsel I received from him has been on relationships. How to nurture them with love while knowing that our loved ones still

have to go through the karmic lessons qualified for them over several lifetimes. My relations have become so much lighter after learning how to practice this. I am ever so grateful to him for this, and many other insights. And I wish him the very best for his first book. It is sure to positively impact many more lives!

—Lavina Tarani, Ex Associate Vice President, RBL Bank, Mumbai

ACKNOWLEDGMENTS

I am thankful and grateful to my son, Gautam Wahi, for all his love and affection, pushing and prodding me to write. And for his help in proof reading, editing and his helpful suggestions in every aspect of the book.

I am indebted to my siblings for their loving support and confidence in me.

I am also thankful to my niece, Saba Siddique, for her constant motivation and helpful suggestions.

I am very thankful to the Partridge Publishing team- Kathy Lorenzo, Vanessa Dean and others for their professional help in publishing, marketing and distribution of the book.

INTRODUCTION

Fourteen or fifteen years back, I was asked to take a workshop with midlevel managers of one of the biggest and most popular malls of Mumbai. I chose success as the subject of that workshop. I began with this question: "Is there anyone in the room who doesn't want to be successful?" Of course, no hands were raised! Then I asked each one of them what success meant to them. One said it would mean being the CEO of that mall. Another said to own a penthouse in South Mumbai. Yet another said for him it was to have a weekend home in Goa. One of them wanted to own a custom-built sports car. One manager wanted to own her own marketing company, and yet another, a chain of retail stores and so on.

After we had done that exercise, I told them that everything they had wanted depended on having more money, position, and power. Did that mean that everyone who has more money or power is happy? After some healthy discussion, all of them agreed that money or power couldn't guarantee happiness. And that though all of them wanted something seemingly different, ultimately whatever they wanted was for that feeling of happiness! And then I asked them, "Would I be wrong if I say being successful means being happy for all of you?" And they all smiled!

For more than two decades, I have been sharing these thoughts of mine with family and friends and in corporate workshops. Finally, I have decided to put some of these thoughts in the form of a book—with the hope that it would motivate and help others to lead abundant lives! If your goal is to get rich quick, this is not the book for you. But if you want to lead a happy, healthy, and fulfilling life with least struggle and heartburn—anytime, anywhere—this book has the potential to change your life!

It is so simple to be happy. It is so simple to be joyous. It is simple to lead abundant lives. To be happy and blissful is our very nature!

But we get so lost or rather caught up
in our environment,
in the frantic nervous energy all around us,
that we completely forget what
our initial desires,
needs, plans, and aspirations were.

We are running, but we have forgotten why and what our intended goal was! The environment all around us is like that, and it is so difficult to get untangled from this mad, mad web, this madness matrix!

We are led to believe that we will be happy when we get that big job. We are led to believe that we will be happy when we move into that big house and get that big car. We think we will be happy when we get the partner or the spouse of our dreams, and we keep chasing the mirage! This is a never-ending marathon in which the bulk of humanity is lost and struggling. What is saddening is that it is so very simple to be successful. Most of humanity is driven by or is running after money, power, and sex. But these can never ever give us abundant lives.

> *Abundant life is when we have optimum health, wealth, relationships, work we love, peace, and joy.*

Most of the things that we think will bring us happiness depend on having more money—the bigger house, the bigger car, exotic vacations, good education, and so on. And that is the root cause of our unhappiness and the reason we feel so unfulfilled and unsuccessful at times!

> *Abundant life is when we begin to experience that all our needs have always been and shall always be fulfilled.*

Money isn't a bad thing. It is not bad as long as we use it as a tool. Problem starts when we start to worship money and make it our god. Yes, lack of money and poverty are not exciting! I often heard my father say,

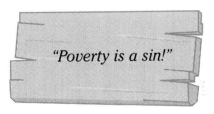

"Poverty is a sin!"

It is true that lack of money can be extremely challenging and it can suck, but still, it is not the god we make it out to be!

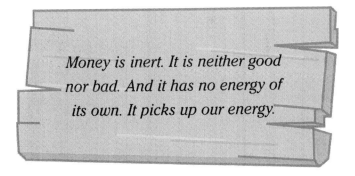

Money is inert. It is neither good nor bad. And it has no energy of its own. It picks up our energy.

If we are the happy kinds, more money will give us more happiness. If we are the unhappy kind, more money will give us more unhappiness. There are hundreds of stories of the superrich and the famous committing suicides or ending up in mental asylums.

> *If you are* happy *with an income of, say, $50,000, you will be* happier *with $500,000 and* happiest *with $5,000,000! But if you are* unhappy *with $50,000, you will be* unhappier *with $500,000 and* unhappiest *with $5,000,000!*

Most of us don't know this and keep running after the mirage called happiness but getting unhappier and more unfulfilled with every raise in our income, with every new possession, and with every passing year!

I was working in New Delhi in the '80s. Being the capital and a mega metro, it was filled with all kinds: persons in government jobs and in the private sector, professionals, and a big trading community. I realized that very few persons were genuinely happy and led fulfilling lives. Eight out of ten managers were unhappy because they were not general managers. Eight general managers were unhappy because they were not vice presidents, and eight VPs were unhappy because they were not presidents! And eight presidents were unhappy that they were not presidents or CEOs of bigger businesses! If not downright unhappy, most of them were certainly not exuberant and joyous!

A happy manager *is a* happier general manager *and the* happiest CEO*! An unhappy manager is an unhappier general manager and the unhappiest CEO!*

It is so true that all the so-called successful people are not always happy, but every happy person is always successful! Because whatever we want to do or possess or achieve is for this *feeling of happiness*!

The cause of our misery is that we are putting the cart before the horse! The forces that want us to remain unhappy, unhealthy, and unfulfilled have blurred our life view! If we become happy without consuming their products and services, they will be lost. So they keep selling us bigger and bigger dreams that shall never satisfy us in the long run, and we shall go to our graves still looking for that elusive happiness!

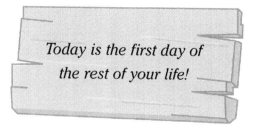

Our competition should only be with our own selves. We should be happier today than we were yesterday. We should be more peaceful *today than we were yesterday. We should be* more joyous *today than we were yesterday!*

It is never too late to learn and to change, and it is simple to lead abundant lives!

Today is the first day of the rest of your life!

In the last three decades or so, I have learned much from my own struggles, love for my family and friends, and watching their struggles and their successes and failures. What I have learned is that all of us can easily create our own House of Abundance and that this house is supported on four pillars!

PILLAR 1 – HAPPINESS

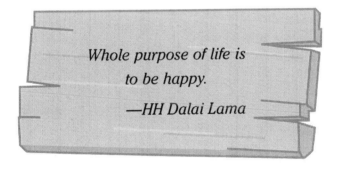

Whole purpose of life is
to be happy.

—HH Dalai Lama

The first and perhaps the most important pillar and the first building block of our House of Abundance is happiness! We hold the key to happiness in our own hands. Whenever we desire, we can open the door and enter the storehouse of joy, inspiration, and strength. Our thoughts can make us unhappy, or they can expand our whole life and fill it with radiant joy.

When we cease to run after passing things and seek within, we never fail to find joy. Then whatever we touch, it blossoms!

When we decide to be happy—happy whatever life may throw at us and however badly people may treat us—our lives change. As I had said earlier, all the so-called successful people aren't happy but every happy person is successful. For we do everything to be happy. Never let anyone, any circumstance, and any situation take your happiness and peace away!

Happiness is simply a decision! You are as happy as you decide to be!

It is not easy in the beginning, but once we become conscious of it and we begin to practice, it becomes a habit and makes it easy for us to be happy—always!

Paramahansa Yogananda had written in his *Autobiography of a Yogi*, more than seven decades back, that all matter is simply energy— be they solids, liquids, or gases! And he had written that "I am telling this to you now, science will tell you this later!" Scientists are now talking of God particle, and it has become common knowledge that everything in the world is energy! Building blocks of the universe are the same—whether these be the stars and galaxies, the oceans and the seas, the houses we live in, the cars we drive, the mobiles and laptops we use, or the food we eat! The only difference in all these is the rate or frequency of their vibration!

All this talk about frequencies and energies is pretty common knowledge today. What is not commonly understood though is that our thoughts affect this energy and vibration.

If we keep breaking it down, all matter is composed of atoms, molecules, electrons and protons, subatomic atoms, and even finer subatomic clouds. All pure energy and our thoughts have a very intimate relationship with this energy! Rishis or saints of India have said millennia ago that all creation is merely an idea in the mind of God, just his thought! And many modern-day thinkers and philosophers and saints agree to that. I have no doubt about it whatsoever.

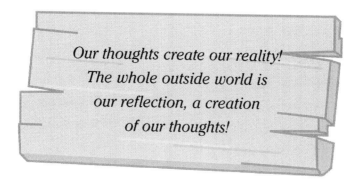

Our thoughts create our reality!
The whole outside world is
our reflection, a creation
of our thoughts!

You just need to work on your thoughts. Your thoughts should only be of happiness and joy, of beauty and love, and of kindness and compassion. And from that base, that energy of joy and happiness, go after your material dreams and desires—a house, a car, a life partner, a business, or a job! And you would see your cup of happiness begin to fill and eventually overflow!

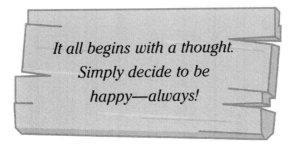

It all begins with a thought. Simply decide to be happy—always!

Happiness Stealers

Unfulfilled *desires* and worrying about the *future* are two major causes of our unhappiness or stealers of our happiness. If we want to be happy and thus successful, we need to understand and deal with both these.

Desires

One day I was talking to Anita, my wife, about the message from Lord Krishna as well as Buddha that desires are the root cause of our suffering. And she told me that it was not possible to live without any desires, and does that mean that we would never be happy? She was a very loving and kind person; she was spiritually inclined and also very pragmatic! I tried to explain to her this concept of desires and happiness with this equation:

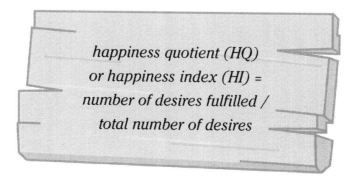

happiness quotient (HQ) or happiness index (HI) = number of desires fulfilled / total number of desires

The idea is not to become desireless—none of us is a saint! But to increase our HQ by striving toward fulfilling all our worthy desires and at the same time keep working toward reducing the total number of our desires—or at the very least, not keep increasing our desires!

But unfortunately, what happens in the market-driven, consumerist society is that by the time we fulfill some of our desires, many more get added, and we keep wondering why we aren't happy!

I told Anita that the trick was to simplify our lives—work on both the numerator as well as the denominator at the same time. And if you keep doing it consistently, one day the numerator and denominator would become the same—that is, you have fulfilled all your desires—and you would be supremely happy.

The idea is to keep life simple. Have ambitions and goals and the urge to improve your situation but don't get drowned in the waters of your own desires!

Ideally have one major desire or goal at one time. With too many desires, our energy and focus get dissipated and distorted. Make sure that your desire is uplifting and legitimate and that it is not harmful or destructive. Having done that, use all your willpower and resources to accomplish that desire, that ambition. Do not leave one task midway to start another. With every success and with every desire and ambition fulfilled, you would become happier, more confident, and more successful!

> *If your desire and your focus is happiness and not mere accumulation of things and stuff, your whole life would begin to expand and grow!*

We all know that the good things in life are very expensive—designer clothes, branded goods, gourmet food, exotic holidays, luxury cars, and so on! But most of the time, we forget that the best things in life are free—a child's smile, a hug or a call from a friend, a sunrise or sunset, a walk in the park, a cool breeze, and so on! Spending time with loved ones and children, being with happy people, spending time in nature—all make us happy and fill us with positive creative energy!

Look for happiness in small day-to-day stuff and activities rather than waiting for big moments and events in your life. Remember that money and possessions are inert. They pick up your energy!

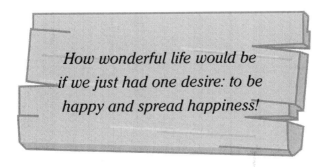

How wonderful life would be if we just had one desire: to be happy and spread happiness!

Remain happy and joyous, and from that base of happiness, look to fulfill all your worthy dreams and desires! You will see that the whole of nature will conspire to help you to become successful!

I recall a very interesting incidence. It was in 2005, and I was the program manager of a major project in Mumbai, India. It was for an oil refinery, and we were doing their business process automation. During the project, we had to take the services of a specialist from Australia.

One fine morning, I picked this Australian up from his hotel to take him for the meeting.

The meeting was near the docks, where the customer had the project site. There were many roadside hutments on the way to the meeting place. On that day, while driving past one of these, the Australian consultant asked the driver to stop all of a sudden. There were some semiclad children playing on the pavement. He watched them intently for a while and then asked me, with an incredulous look on his face, "What are they happy about?"

> *The children were barefoot and wearing rags, and they were playing happily. They were laughing. They had no care in the world.*

We really do not need much to be happy! It is so unfortunate that we measure the success or importance of a country by its gross domestic product (GDP), while it should be GHI—gross happiness index!

Do whatever makes you happy. Study the subjects that make you happy, the ones you love studying. Look for work and hobbies that make you happy. Make your passion your work or your business! If not workable just now, choose to be happy doing whatever you need to do; cribbing and whining about it would make things worse. Make friends with happy souls and keep away from negativity!

Anita, my beautiful and talented wife, barely passed her high school, as mathematics and science were not her cup of tea! In college, she took fine arts and topped all through, including her masters in music! I was a reluctant and unhappy design engineer but a happy and successful sales manager because I loved traveling and meeting people!

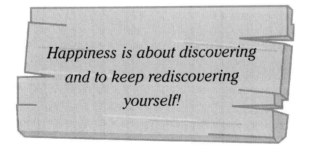

Happiness is about discovering and to keep rediscovering yourself!

Past and Future

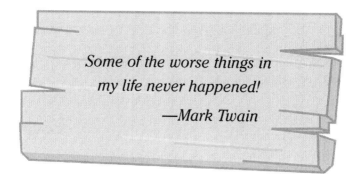

*Some of the worse things in
my life never happened!*
—*Mark Twain*

The second major cause of our unhappiness, other than unfulfilled desires, is worrying about the future. And it is so true that most of the things we worry about never happen!

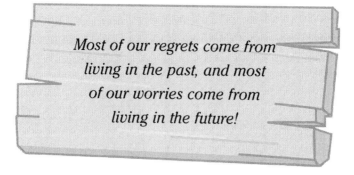

*Most of our regrets come from
living in the past, and most
of our worries come from
living in the future!*

And both these, regrets of the past and worries of the future, rob us of our happiness. And they also deplete our energies, without in any way, helping us become healthier, happier, and successful!

> *Why live on the broken pieces of yesterday?*

> *Never dwell on any negative or sad incidences of the past. Learn the lesson but forget the incidence! Remember and dwell only on the happy memories of the past!*

Most of the things we worry about in the future never happen, but they do rob our present of its happiness and peace. We should and we must take common sense measures, but we should not live in the future. Planning for the future is not the same as living in the future.

Let us say you are thinking of investing in a house of your own and are concerned about the mortgage. Look at your income and major expenses. See what is important and what is not; look at what all you can do without for a few years. And remember that under normal circumstances, your income would keep growing but the mortgage would be fixed. After a few years, you would be in a comfortable position. After having looked at all the options, you may decide to go ahead or postpone buying a property to a later date or look for a different location. This is planning and preparing and making rational choices.

Living in the future on the other hand is, What will happen if I lose my job? How will I manage if there is a recession in the economy? What will happen if I get transferred to another city or country? Such thoughts are our happiness stealers and energy sappers. Every tomorrow will come as today only. Do your best and let go!

On a lighter note—talking of buying property—we have had some of the best years of our lives in small rented houses!

> *Today, the now, is the only reality, and it is our* responsibility *and our* duty *to remain* happy *and* peaceful *and to live* mindfully!

Other than these two major happiness stealers, there are a few others that look very innocuous or something we cannot do without but are very capable of causing a lot of unhappiness!

One is news. I had stopped reading newspapers and watching news on TV more than a decade back! They thrive on selling negativity. I still get most of the important news. Keeping us informed and getting immersed in news/negativity are two different things.

I am reminded of an interesting incidence. In 2014, I had gone to Los Angeles to attend our annual World Convocation.[1] It was a very uplifting time with many discourses, group meditations and visits to peaceful retreats. There were more than four thousand of us from about forty countries. I had the last day free to myself, and my flight was at night. I was enjoying a cup of tea on a beautiful August morning in a café near my hotel in Downtown Los Angeles, and a well-built

---

[1]   SRF (Self-Realization Fellowship) / Yogoda Satsanga Society of India was established by Paramahansa Yogananda a century ago and has its HQ in Los Angeles, California. Members/devotees from all over the world get together every year in what is called World Convocation.

American male came and took the table next to mine. After a few minutes, he looked at me and asked in a strong, loud voice, "Did you hear the radio at night? What do you think of the situation in Syria? Where the hell is the world going?"

I smiled and said, "I don't even know where I am going and you are asking me where the world is going!"

He kept quiet for a while and then said, "You look very happy and peaceful. What do you do?" I told him about the Self-Realization Fellowship and our convocation. And he said it sounded good and he would surely check it out. I hope he did, because we are living in more challenging times today than we were in 2014!

Media sensationalizes every bit of news, and it is repeated so much that it is bound to affect our thoughts and feelings!

Another thing that steals our happiness is negative people around us—could be family, friends, or coworkers. I know it is not easy to wish away negative people from our lives. But once we become conscious that they are affecting our energy and making us unhappy and restless, we shall find ways and means to reduce the interaction or make us more resilient—and eventually be able to convert them into happy and positive persons like our own selves! We have no control over what others do, but how we respond to them is entirely in our hands!

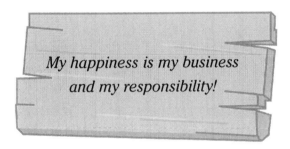

My happiness is my business and my responsibility!

Happiness Enhancers

Like happiness stealers, there are happiness enhancers too, and these can make our lives happier and enriching. Two vital happiness enhancers are *curiosity* and *enthusiasm*!

> *Curiosity might have killed the cat, but it brings life and zest into our otherwise stagnant, listless lives!*

One should be curious about life and its processes. Curiosity is the ability to seek and acquire new knowledge, skills, and ways of understanding the world we live in.

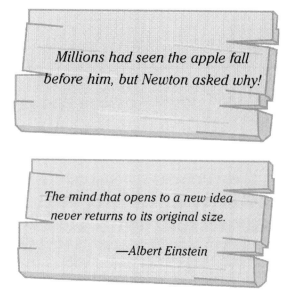

> *Millions had seen the apple fall before him, but Newton asked why!*

> *The mind that opens to a new idea never returns to its original size.*
>
> —*Albert Einstein*

Curiosity is what keeps us learning and growing throughout our life. And the more we learn and grow, the happier we are!

Blessed are the curious
They learn
They grow
They evolve!

Happiest are the curious
Learning never exhausts their minds
They are always
Fresh and alive!
A curious pairs of eyes
Can lead us to
The elixir of life!

Every morning, get up with a smile! Do not leave the bed until you have smiled to yourself!

Do things that make you happy and do them with enthusiasm. Even if the only thing that makes you happy is that cup of tea or coffee! Make it with enthusiasm. Make it a ritual. Buy beautiful teapots and coffee mugs! Buy a tea timer! Buy the best coffee and the most exotic teas that you can!

> *If the single-celled microbe, the first form of life on earth, was not enthusiastic, life might have remained just that: single-celled!*

Without curiosity and enthusiasm, life becomes routine, dull, and listless—a sure recipe for an unhappy and unfilled life.

Catching Them Young

For the past few years, Delhi government schools have been in the news a lot. The entire education system has been completely revamped, and I understand that the new model of education is already a subject of research in a couple of institutes/universities in the UK and USA. One of the new initiatives in this new model is happiness! Happiness curriculum was introduced in the schools run by Delhi State Government, and fittingly, HH Dalai Lama inaugurated it!

I have no doubt that the students who will come out of these schools will be relatively more successful in life and will be better equipped to face the world and its challenges!

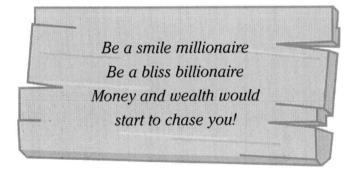

Be a smile millionaire
Be a bliss billionaire
Money and wealth would
start to chase you!

Suggested Actions

1. When you wake up in the morning, first thing you should do is smile! Do not leave your bed till you have smiled. Whenever you find yourself serious or unhappy or angry during the day, take a deep breath and smile!

2. Practice the following affirmation[2] before sleeping at night: I am happy, healthy, and wealthy. My life is filled with love, joy, and laughter.

3. Write down your most important goal in life, and look at it and think about it once a day. See what you can do that day to get closer to its fulfillment.

4. Make a list of small day-to-day things that make you happy. Do as many of those as often as you can.

---

[2]   The right way of using affirmations is to first say them aloud a couple of times then in a murmur a couple of times and mentally a few times in the end.

PILLAR 2 – GRATITUDE

We don't realize how fortunate we are. But for God's grace, you and I could have been living in that slum, that hutment, my Australian colleague saw!

Once we are happy, gratefulness comes to us naturally. We start to thank God for all his blessings. And the more we thank him, the more he gives. God/nature will start to give us more and more reasons to be grateful for, and we will become happier. We would have put in motion an ever-increasing cycle of abundance.

And we need to be grateful for our pain and suffering too—these, too, are his gifts. At times—in fact, most of the time—these are our best teachers!

I like this story: A saintly teacher and few of his students were living in a quiet hamlet near a river. One day, one of the students asked the teacher, "If God is so loving and everything is his creation, why did he create so much pain and suffering?" The teacher did not reply, but he took the hand of the student in his own hand and started to walk toward the river. There was a boat on the banks, and it had two oars. The teacher took the student with him to the boat and pushed it gently into the river stream. Once they were midstream, the teacher started to use one oar, and the boat started to swirl at the same place. The student kept watching for a while, seeing the boat just swirling in the same place. The thought that maybe the teacher was getting forgetful in his old age or his other arm was hurt, came into his mind. But he waited obediently for a while and then asked the teacher, "Sir, why aren't you using both the oars? Do you need my help?"

And the teacher said, "Just like this boat can't move forward with one oar, our lives, too, need two oars to move forward—pleasure and pain, joy and suffering!"

One cannot be happy and it is very difficult to be grateful when we are in pain, when there is suffering, and when there is lack. But when we start to become more aware of life and its processes and when we start to understand the higher principles and spiritual laws that govern our lives, it becomes easier. Start doing it, and you will experience it too, like I did.

I am not talking about being happy when there is suffering. It is about being at peace within us, in our hearts. There is no end to suffering. Be thankful for your lot; it could have been worse. Remember, whole of life is cyclic.

Nothing lasts! If good times did not last, bad won't too. Night is the darkest and the coldest before dawn! Once our perceptions and our attitudes change, the mighty forces of nature come in to help. All of life is governed by karma and by cause and effect—action and reaction!

A couple of months back, I had gone to meet a niece of mine. She is a young mother, and I am very fond of the whole family. She has had a peculiar health challenge, but on the whole, she is very active and enjoying life. Her whole family is loving and supportive, and they are very well off!

I had been sending her healing and called her up one day. Listening to her, I felt she would start to heal now. A couple of days after the call, I had an inner urge to go and see her. She was looking good and happy. She told me that she was feeling better but was feeling bad that she was still not able to pursue her passion! She was wondering why this had happened to her. When she said that, all of a sudden, I remembered my friend Jain and told her his story.[3]

In the late '70s, just some months after his marriage, Jain met with an accident. He was on his way to the office on a scooter with another common friend of ours. The other friend was driving, but the truck hit Jain's right thigh directly, and it became like a pulp! The next two to three years were spent in and out of hospitals, and his first son was born when he was still in the hospital.[4]

He survived, but he was walking on crutches. The organization we were working for was very understanding and gave him a simple desk job. I left that job and the city in 1981 and moved to Delhi, but we remained in touch. Physically, things became more difficult for him over the years; but mentally and spiritually, he kept getting stronger with every passing year!

---

[3]   Quite a few fresh engineering graduates had joined the same organization in Ranchi, India, at the same time in 1971–72! Jain and I were among them. It was here that I was an unhappy or unsuccessful design engineer, mentioned earlier!

[4]   His wife was expecting when he had the accident.

He had to undergo many more surgeries in the years that followed, and finally, both his legs had to be amputated. He took voluntary retirement about twenty years back and moved to another city, Lucknow, where his wife had some relations. He had spent most of the past forty years in and out of hospitals and the last fifteen odd years in his bed and had never gone out. Hats off not only to him but to his wife too, who had spent her entire married life in and out of hospitals and looking after her husband!

> The moment I had started narrating this story, my niece had tears in her eyes, and my eyes got wet too. And I realized that she would be completely healed soon. She had got her lesson—to be grateful; there is no end to sorrow and suffering!

And strangely, when I was telling her the story, I too, felt healed. I felt so light, as if a heavy load had been lifted from my heart!

I had visited the Jains some years back and stayed a night with them. He was as cheerful as he used to be forty years back, before his accident. And so was his wife!

Just imagine being stuck to one bed for fifteen years with a very active mind! Every night for the last fifteen odd years, his wife had been giving him the same dinner—khichdi (rice and lentils dish), as it was easier to digest! And Jain told me with a smile, "Partner, there is no problem! Life is good! I have two phones[5] and can talk to all my friends anytime! And the best thing is that I have control over the TV remote!"

One Mr. Gupta used to come to their house at about ten every morning to help Jain. Gupta would help clean him up, give him some massage (to give the body some movement for digestion), make tea; they would have tea together and talk. Gupta would spend two to three hours with him and leave.

During this lockdown[6] period, I have been calling up friends and relations regularly. One day I called up Jain, and he was as chirpy as ever! I knew lockdown is irrelevant for him, as

---

[5]   Both are landlines; he still doesn't own a mobile!

[6]   * COVID-19

he has been under this for decades! I came to know that Gupta was not able to come to his place during the lockdown. I told Jain that as this was a genuine need, he could get permission for Gupta to come. I was bowled over by his answer! Just imagine a person who has spent more than forty years in and out of hospitals and more than fifteen years in bed—when I told him that he could get permission for Gupta to come, he said, "No, partner. God wants me to become stronger!" My eyes are wet even now when I am writing this.

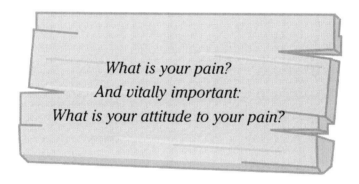

What is your pain?
And vitally important:
What is your attitude to your pain?

You know it is relatively easier to say which was our happiest day—the day I got my first bike, the day I got my degree or my first job, the day I got engaged or married, the day I got my first house, my first car, or my first child, whatever! But there is no end to suffering and sorrow. It could always have been worse. So we need to thank God for our pain and suffering too. Thank God that it is just this much and no more!

Let us be grateful that we are alive! I challenge you to take a piece of paper and write down all the things that are good in your life, things you are grateful for, and also the pains and challenges of your life. You will see that the good things list is always bigger. If it is not, I am sure you haven't noted the many gifts and blessings we take for granted!

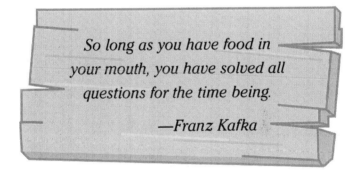

So long as you have food in your mouth, you have solved all questions for the time being.

—Franz Kafka

I remember decades back when I got my first AC car in Delhi, I used to thank God all the time in my long ride to work in the hot Delhi summer. I used to thank him equally for the hot water in our bath in the winters. We take all these so much for granted!

I think it was this trait of mine, being thankful and grateful, that helped me through a very difficult period of my life in the '90s. Let me share this story, as this also illustrates cyclicity[7] of life!

My first AC car, which I have mentioned above, was during the time I was working with HCL, and I used to drive down to Noida from Greater Kailash in New Delhi, more than twenty kilometers. Things had become very difficult for me in that organization, and I was desperately looking for a change. Luckily, I got a senior management role in a MNC, and we moved to Pune. But unfortunately, Anita had to leave the work she was doing (she had her own music and painting classes).

Luckily, our son got admission in a good engineering college in Pune, and we also bought our first apartment there. I was doing well in my new job, and everything looked great! But after a year or so, for the first time in our two-decade-old married life, we had some problems.

---

[7] I had used this word in my blog last year but couldn't find it in standard dictionaries! Maybe it would be included one of these days! I like it!

In hindsight, it is very easy to say, "Could have said that" or "Could have done this" and so on. This was in the mid-'90s. Before joining HCL, I was working in Gillette in Delhi in the late '80s, and we were known as the "made for each other" couple! We never fought. We were supposed to be the happiest and most well-adjusted couple in our family and circle of friends!

This led to a lot of learning for me in the years to come, and I learned some very valuable life-enhancing lessons. One of these was this: I thought to myself, *If we, who are supposed to be made for each other, can have problems, what about the rest of the world?* And I realized this:

> *However happy, however affluent, however good a family may appear, if we dig deeper, if we go behind the facade, we will find that every family has some challenges. These could be financial, health, or relationships—anything!*

All this made me introspect, and looking back, this is the period I started to realize life is not what it appears to be! I also learned that more money, corporate perks, or higher status don't necessarily mean we would be happier. I became more spiritual and realized that most people turn to God only when they have had to face some serious challenges or tragedies in life!

But maybe I had not learned my lesson fully, and life gave me another opportunity to suffer and learn. If I were a fast learner or if I were smart, I might have been saved from further pain. But that was not to be.

From Pune, I moved to Mumbai as CEO of a logistics company. I think it was both: more money and ego—lure of higher status! It took me a couple of years to realize more vividly that possessions and money cannot guarantee happiness and that there is no end to pain and suffering!

I quit my job and the corporate rat race on October 9, 1998. I was under debt, I had no savings,[8] our son had done his engineering but

---

[8] Mortgage for the Pune apartment and whatever was there had gone in buying the apartment.

didn't have a job, and my wife hadn't started to work as yet.

Company house and company car and driver had gone, and we had to move to a smaller apartment. I was traveling in buses and Mumbai locals—Mumbai's lifeline those years! And yet I was happy and at peace. The whole load of proving something to the world was gone! And I thanked God for the pain and the suffering of the last few years—which had paved the way and prepared the ground for deeper and more enduring happiness that was not dependent on any material thing![9]

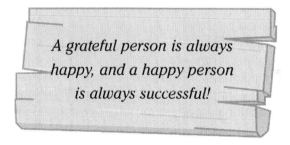

A grateful person is always happy, and a happy person is always successful!

---

[9]   With the grace of God, soon I was able to earn even more than I used to and without any stress or strain!

Suggested Actions

1. Make a list of good things and blessings in your life, things you are grateful for. Add to this list as more good things come in your life. Read this list as often as possible but minimum of once every week.

2. Make a habit of thanking your family and friends and coworkers for everything they do for you, however small.

3. Thank God for everything, every day in your prayers.

PILLAR 3 – GIVING

I am happy when good
things happen to me.
I am equally happy when good
things happen to others.
But I am the happiest when good
things happen to others through me!

I am sure most of us have experienced this in our lives—that we are happier when we do things for others, by being kind to others. I wonder why we forget it. Why don't we do it more often? Why don't we do it all the time!

> *All lasting wealth comes*
> *from enriching others*
> *in some way.*

Years ago, anthropologist Margaret Mead was asked by a student what she considered to be the first sign of civilization in a culture. The student expected Mead to talk about fishhooks or clay pots or grinding stones. But Mead said that the first sign of civilization in an ancient culture was a femur (thighbone) that had been broken and then healed. Mead explained that in the animal kingdom, if you break your leg, you die. You cannot run from danger, get to the river for a drink, or hunt for food. You are meat for prowling beasts. No animal survives a broken leg long enough for the bone to heal.

> *"A broken femur that has healed is evidence that someone has taken time to stay with the one who fell, has bound up the wound, has carried the person to safety, and has tended the person through recovery. Helping someone else through difficulty is where civilization starts," Mead said.*

When I had read the above in a blog, I was immediately reminded of Jain, for he had broken his femur! When Jain was in and out of hospitals, friends looked after him and his family all the time. Years later, he told us one day that if he had such an accident in Delhi, his hometown, he would have died. It was only the love and care of his friends that saved him.

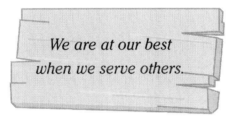

We are at our best when we serve others.

I am reminded of another beautiful story I had read ages back in a small book—*Your Life Your Choice*! It had described serving others and getting it back through a simple tale. In this tale, the inhabitants of heaven as well as hell were served the same food on similar dining tables and similar very long spoons. They were not supposed to eat with their hands and were to use the spoons only. The ones in heaven were happy and healthy, but those in hell were dying of hunger. The inhabitants of hell were not able to eat, as the spoons were too long. But the inhabitants of heaven were feeding each other across the table with the long spoons!

> *And ultimately, I think, that is the only purpose of life: to be able to help others and to serve others. Heaven and hell are our own creation!*

Whenever someone comes to me for any help, I take it as a *window of opportunity*! I call it WOO! I know that even if I do nothing, that person will still survive and get what is due to him. I will be the loser, as that WOO will go to someone else!

> *When we are happy and grateful, giving becomes easy. And the more we give, the more we get.*

Giving is perhaps the most potent of the spiritual laws of success. What we want, we need to give. If we want love, we need to give love. If we want respect and appreciation, we need to give respect and appreciation. If we want money, we need to give money!

> *As we give generously to others, nature will multiply those seeds in our own life in return!*

We should give our best, and we should give generously. In other words, stretch yourself. Go out of your way.

> *Once we understand enough is enough, we realize that we have more than enough. That is abundance!*

I encourage you to look for ways to give generously and meet the needs of others. Don't leave it for tomorrow. Start today!

You can't help everyone, but you can always help someone. You could be the answer to someone's prayers.

Remember, people have many different types of needs. There may be someone who needs some encouragement. Give generously when you give that encouragement. There may be someone in your life who just needs a friend; they need some quality time. Give generously of your time.

Let me share another life-changing or rather life-enhancing experience of mine. It is from the time I was working with Gillette in the late '80s. We had a colleague who was very proud of his children. He used to talk often to us about them, especially his daughter. Unfortunately, he died rather young, and the family was in financial trouble. I met our HR head, who was very senior to me, and suggested that the organization should do something for the family, like giving his wife a job. But he refused, citing company policy and rules. I tried my best to persuade him to do something, but he didn't agree. Finally, I told him that in that case, I would see what I, myself, could do to help the family. He told me that I was getting too emotional and that there were hundreds of thousands suffering like this family. And he questioned my ability to be able to help all. I shared with him a saying of Helen Keller:[10]

> *"I am one person and I cannot do everything. But just because I can't do everything doesn't mean I would refuse to do that, which I can."*

---

[10] My father had presented me with her biography when I was still in school in the mid-'60s—God bless his soul!

With God's grace, and a little help and lots of love from me, everything turned out well for the family. It was such a fulfilling experience for me that I started to consciously look for more opportunities to experience this joy of sharing and giving!

> *Generosity is the most natural outward expression of an inner attitude of compassion and loving-kindness.*
> *—HH Dalai Lama*

The giving principle is true, and it works even at our workplaces and in our jobs and professions.

A typical mindset in the competitive environment of today is, What is in it for me? What do I get? We need to change our thoughts and our attitude to this: What can I do? How can I serve, and how can I help? The moment we make this shift in our mindsets, in our psyche, this happens:

> *Every thought and every act of ours becomes sanctified and is bound to bring abundance!*

This works, and I have seen the results so clearly over and over again. Spiritual laws work as unerringly as physical laws. Even if you don't know what gravity is, the moment you step into space from a height, you are going to fall! Similarly, we may not know the laws of giving and gratitude, but they still work as unerringly as gravity!

> *God is love, and service is the active expression of that love.*

The more we practice giving and serving, the happier we are. And we begin to realize that this happiness is much deeper and more fulfilling than the normal happiness that comes from doing pleasurable things. It is so fulfilling that we begin to look for more and opportunities to help, to serve, to WOO!

> *Happiness is like a butterfly—the more*
> *you chase it, more it will elude you.*
> *And when you turn your attention*
> *on other things, it will come and*
> *quietly sit on your shoulder!*
>
> *—David Henry Thoreau*

So our happiness and gratitude cycle of abundance gets stronger with the addition of the third pillar of giving!

> *The more we give, the happier we will be.*
> *The happier we are, the more*
> *grateful we will be!*
> *The more grateful we are,*
> *the more we will give!*
> *And that is true abundance!*

Having said that, I know giving is not as simple as being happy and grateful. In fact, it is our mind that makes giving complex. How much to give? When to give? Whom to give? And so on!

Like everything else in life, there are no hard-and-fast rules about this. There can't be, as every individual and every situation is so unique. We need wisdom to be able to make right choices. Most religions and communities have their guidelines. Many families have their traditions and customs. I believe once we have this desire to serve and to give, all answers begin to come.

When to Give

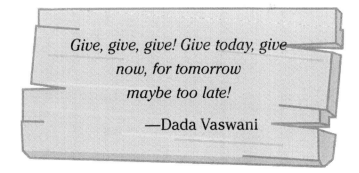

Give, give, give! Give today, give now, for tomorrow maybe too late!

—Dada Vaswani

I have heard about an incident from the Indian epic *Mahabharata*: Yudhisthira, the wise and benevolent king, asks a beggar seeking alms to come the next day. On hearing this, Bhima, his younger brother, rejoices that Yudhisthira, his brother, has conquered death! For he is sure that he will be around tomorrow to give.

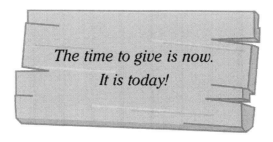

The time to give is now. It is today!

How Much to Give?

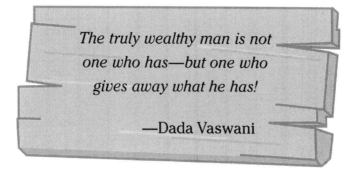

The truly wealthy man is not one who has—but one who gives away what he has!

—Dada Vaswani

In India, we have a custom of giving money as a gift on auspicious occasions, like marriages, birth of a child, housewarming, etc. (it is still there but is changing). And the amount varies with one's means and the closeness of relation or friendship. Many times Anita would ask me whether to give X amount or Y, and I would tell her, "When in doubt, give the higher amount. While giving, to err on the side of more is wiser!"

I recollect another incident with my wife. At times, I used to enjoy poking her with my concepts, but it was always done in a lighthearted manner!

Once, she was a little upset with me giving away too much and mentioned this proverb: "Cut your coat according to your cloth!" It was at a point in our lives when we were really struggling to make both ends meet—so to say![11]

I knew what she meant, and she had a point. But I told her, "No, that won't work. If I cut the coat according to my cloth, it may not fit me. I will not be able to wear it! I would rather give that piece of cloth to someone needy whom it

---

[11] This was in 1998–99 when I had quit my job and had very little income.

will fit, and the universe will give me the right size and the right fit at the right time!"

Whatever our income, we should first take out a percentage for charity (the amount is our choice, but it should be practiced consistently), and next comes saving. After that, one should spend joyously without any worries and with an open heart!

I have observed an interesting thing while working with seniors in India. And that is this: Many of them, rather most of them, neither spend money on themselves—for their comforts and hobbies—nor do they do much charity, and they leave everything for their children. And their children either don't need it by that time or waste it away. They haven't earned it, so they don't know its value or its worth. Sad, isn't it?

Charity does begin at home! Do give to your children first, but give them when you are alive. Give them when they need it. Give to other relations or friends who need it. Give to the causes you support.

> *What you leave behind was never yours. What you spent, you had, and what you gave away goes with you!*

It is not how much one gives but how one gives that really matters. You can give anything, but you must give from your heart and give willingly and lovingly!

What to Give

It is not only money that can be given. It could be a flower or even a smile. In fact, my experience is that giving money is the easiest thing in the world and, arguably, least important! As I wrote earlier, we need to give what we want! Love, appreciation, respect, a compliment—whatever you want, you need to give! When you give a smile to a stranger, that may be the only good thing received by him in days and weeks!

> *What is the use of possessing abundant positive energy when we don't spend that energy in service to humanity? We will be like a fully charged battery with open terminals that gets destroyed with time.*

For me for some years now, it has been time. Giving my time is the most expensive gift I can give to anyone. Time is my most precious possession!

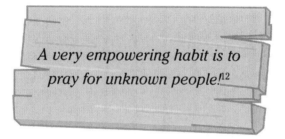

> *A very empowering habit is to pray for unknown people![12]*

Walking in the streets, driving past someone, a passenger sitting next to you, patients in a hospital—wish them well in your heart. Pray for them. Ask God to give them healthy and happy lives! Ask God to lessen their suffering and their

---

[12] Praying for family and friends is natural and a given!

pain. Start to do it regularly, and you will see that your own cup of happiness is overflowing and abundance is pouring in from all sides!

Whom to Give

> *Nothing in nature lives for itself. Rivers do not drink their own water, nor do trees eat their own fruit. Sun doesn't shine for itself and nor do the flowers bloom for their own selves!*

Many times we avoid giving by finding fault with the person who is asking. However, being judgmental and saying no to a person on the presumption that he may not be worthy or the most deserving is not very uplifting. But yes, we do need wisdom and discrimination.

> *The sun shines equally, and the trees give their shade equally to all!*

As I had said earlier, my wife was a giving and loving person and was a firm believer that charity begins at home. Charity does begin at home, but we need to keep expanding our circle of giving!

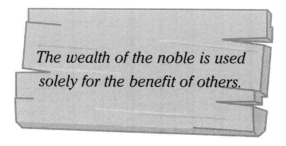

The wealth of the noble is used solely for the benefit of others.

How to Give

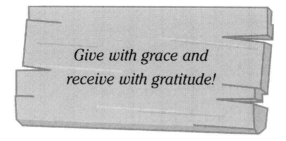

Give with grace and receive with gratitude!

In giving, follow this advice: let not your left hand know what your right hand gives! Charity without publicity and fanfare is the highest form of charity.

While giving, let not the recipient feel small or humiliated. And don't let giving make you proud! Giving and receiving are two sides of the same coin!

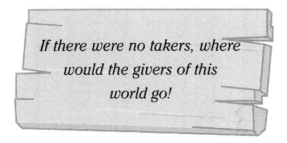

If there were no takers, where would the givers of this world go!

After all, what we give never really belonged to us. We come to this world with nothing and will go with nothing. Whatever we have is a gift from the universe. The thing gifted was only with us for a temporary period. Why then take pride in giving away something that really did not belong to us?

Give and never regret giving!

I would conclude pillar three with a saying of Saint Kabir:

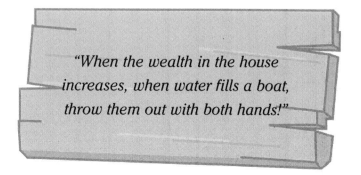

"When the wealth in the house increases, when water fills a boat, throw them out with both hands!"

Suggested Actions

1. Decide a percentage you would like to spend on charity and do it regularly. Doing more than that is always welcome.
2. Say or do something nice and kind to at least one person every day—something that brings a smile in their lives. It doesn't matter how small or big it is.
3. Introspect and see what is most important for you at this point in your life: money, love, respect, time, or anything else. Whatever is the most important thing for you, you must give that very often— preferably every day!

PILLAR 4 – BALANCE

In the science fiction movie *Avatar* (directed beautifully by James Cameron), when the war starts, Jake goes to Eywa (the guiding force and deity of Pandora) and asks for her help. Neytiri tells Jake that Eywa doesn't take sides—it just *protects the balance*!

> *That is what Mother Earth does too! And this is what the universe does: just protects the balance! Nature's nature is balance.*

To lead a happy, abundant, and fulfilling life, it must be balanced. Happiness does depend, to a certain extent, on external conditions but chiefly on our mental attitudes. In order to lead a happy and fulfilling life, one should have good health, balanced mind, work one loves, prosperous life, and wisdom.

> *If the wheel of our life is not balanced, our ride won't be smooth. Even if one spoke is missing in the wheel of a bicycle, it will wobble.*

And so shall our lives if any component is missing. Balance is necessary to lead an abundant life!

> *Success is a ladder up that we go step-by-step. If the ladder isn't balanced, we are sure to fall.*

During the last two to three decades in which I have been coaching and mentoring corporate executives and friends, I have come to realize that many of them have the first three qualities or traits to various degrees. Many of them are *happy* kinds and are very *giving* persons. So many are *happy* and filled with *gratitude*. *Giving* and *gratitude* are natural to many.

> *They are reasonably happy and are satisfied with their lives under normal circumstances. Their lives crumble under serious health and relationship issues, natural disasters, and financial depressions.*

In recent years, the 2008 financial meltdown or depression and COVID-19 are just two examples. This happens because the fourth pillar of the House of Abundance—balance—is missing or not strong enough in their lives.

At every stage of our life, we have a prime driver or responsibility or duty—whatever we may call it. If you are working, your job, your business, or your profession is your prime activity. If you are a student, study is the primary function. If you are a housewife, running the house is your prime activity!

I had got the following chart from a younger friend with whom I had talked about the four pillars of abundant life!

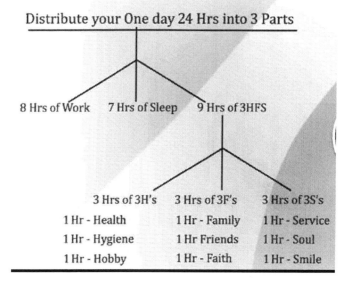

Perfect Maintenance of Life

Distribute your One day 24 Hrs into 3 Parts

8 Hrs of Work	7 Hrs of Sleep	9 Hrs of 3HFS

3 Hrs of 3H's	3 Hrs of 3F's	3 Hrs of 3S's
1 Hr - Health	1 Hr - Family	1 Hr - Service
1 Hr - Hygiene	1 Hr Friends	1 Hr - Soul
1 Hr - Hobby	1 Hr - Faith	1 Hr - Smile

To keep it simple, we could divide the day into three portions of eight hours each. In this, eight hours would be sleep for all. A good night's sleep is not only vital for our health, it makes us happier too. So many studies all around the world have found that a good night's sleep makes us happy. And we have seen that a happy person is a successful person!

A student could do eight hours of study, a working person eight hours of job, and a housewife eight hours of house chores and divide the remaining eight hours in HFS!

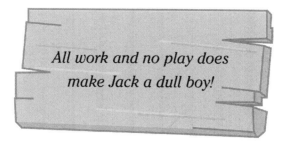

All work and no play does make Jack a dull boy!

But alas! I mostly see sad, overworked, and stressed-out people all around. If not sad, they are not exuberant and joyous. They are so caught up in their environment, in the fast-paced life, that they take their unhappy and unfulfilled state as natural! Most of them work for twelve hours or more every day (including commuting).

And the story of students is similar. Some parents push their children too much. And, of course, some students themselves get caught up in the competitive spirit and lead very unbalanced lives! There's nothing wrong in working hard and nothing wrong in studying hard, but if we are doing it to be able to make more money, to get famous and popular, or to win at any cost, eventually we shall not only be disappointed but also actually get damaged—physically, emotionally, and mentally!

Valorie Kondos Field was the coach of UCLA women's gymnastics team for twenty-nine years, and she led them to many championship victories. What she had said in a TEDx talk is so true and has been my experience for years. She had said, "Winning is really, really fun! But winning doesn't always equal success. In the USA and elsewhere, win-at-all-cost culture is a crisis. In our schools, in our businesses, in our politics; winning at any cost has become acceptable. In society we honour the people at the top of the pyramid. But sadly quite often, those same people are leaving their institutions as damaged human beings—emotionally, mentally and not just physically."

In leading a balanced life, like everything else, there are no hard-and-fast rules. There can't be, as every individual and every situation is so unique. We need wisdom to be able to make right choices!

The HFS given above is a general guideline to make us think. Creative people need less sleep!

Persons doing what they love and are passionate about can happily burn the midnight oil!

> We need to take a break.
> We need to *pause* and *reflect*!
> And we need to ask ourselves *why.*

What we are doing is important but never as important as why!

> *The two most important days in your life are the day you are born and the day you find out why!*
>
> —Mark Twain

We get so caught up in our environment, in the win-at-all-cost culture, that we forget the *why* of what we are doing. We think we are working for the family, but the family may need our time more than the money. And we have seen money does not and cannot make us happy!

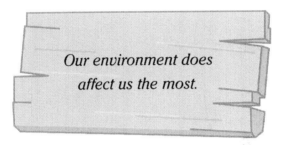

Our environment does affect us the most.

When we get caught up in the environment around us and don't have any time to pause and reflect, two things that are most important in life get most neglected: *family* and *God!*[13]

We are like the bee that refuses to fly away even when the flower starts to close its petals at dusk!

---

[13] Faith/contemplation/meditation/praying

Mind over Matter

> *Unless we have a very strong and centered mind, it is extremely difficult to counter the negative effects of the environment and to remain insulated from its negative or dark energy.*

We keep hearing about the left and right brain. We keep hearing about reason and feeling. Men are from Mars and women are from Venus! It is all about the masculine principle and the feminine principle. And it has been there from the very beginning—right from Adam and Eve! Adam was mostly reason, and Eve was mostly feeling. Both are needed to lead an abundant life. Only reason or feeling and emotions alone will not work. They would lead to inharmonious lives.

Generally speaking, men have more of masculine principle and women more of feminine principle. That is, men usually have more reason and women have more feelings.

All of us have both—reason and feeling or emotions! But some women have more of masculine principle, and some men more of the feminine principle. We can also call these masculine and feminine energies.

To lead an abundant life, we need balance. We need a centered mind or brain. One simple way of doing it is by using our other hand consciously (for right-handed persons, left; and for left-handed persons, right). There are other such ways to bring about some centering, but the most effective way, the best way to center the brain, is *meditation.*

> *"For one who never unites the mind with God/Self there is no peace and wisdom; and how can one who lacks peace be happy?"*[14]

Meditation teaches us focus, concentration, and living in the now! If we meditate for an hour

---

[14] *Bhagavad Gita*, chapter 2, verse 66

a day,[15] it will save at least two hours of study or time at work. We become more productive and more creative. It is a wise investment!

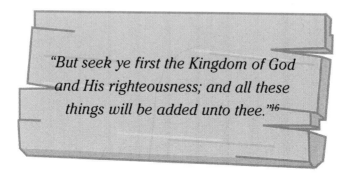

"But seek ye first the Kingdom of God and His righteousness; and all these things will be added unto thee."[16]

This is true, and it works. Over the years, many young people have told me, "We shall look for God or start to meditate when we reach your age!" And they continue to struggle and lead unfulfilled, stressful lives. They don't realize that they would actually save time and perform better if they started now and thus lead more abundant lives!

Worldly people believe that meditative or contemplative people are passive or serious. Nothing could be farther from truth! But I do

---

[15] Ideally half an hour in the morning and half an hour at night

[16] Mathew 6:33

understand where they are coming from. In the beginning of my seeking, I, too, was very serious about my path. But all this changed when I started to meditate regularly! When through contemplation and meditation, we begin to touch the inner and deeper realms, all dullness and seriousness vanishes, and our life is filled with abundant joy!

Swami Vivekananda had said this:

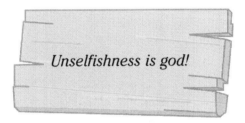

Unselfishness is god!

When we think of others and when we start to go beyond our own self, that is being spiritual, that is being godly, and that is being religious. We can also say godliness is happiness. Inner peace always brings smiles on our faces!

> *Smile is an expression of love, of peace, of joy and flows easily and spontaneously with God's contact. Godliness is happiness!*

If we keep smiling, we will see good and joyous things only!

> *Happy people are usually spiritual, and spiritual people are usually happier!*

Being spiritual also makes us humble. When we realize the infinitude of creation and thus God, we naturally become humble. And it works the other way around too—humble people are normally more spiritual. When we gain access to the spiritual realm, it does not matter what happens in the world. We become indifferent to success and failure, victory and defeat. On the other hand, an ordinary person rises and falls with the changing circumstances.

For most of us, mind is our master.
We need to make it our slave!
Our thoughts create our reality!

A meditative person, a spiritual person, knows nothing lasts. If good times did not last, bad will not too. He is at peace and, with a calm and centered mind, is looking for ways and means to come out of the seemingly difficult situation.

Each problem and each challenge
that awaits a solution in your
hands is a religious duty imposed
on you by life itself. An easy
life is not a victorious life!

Family, Friends, and Faith[17]

I had read a story of John, a carpenter in the US. He was a simple and conscientious person and was very devoted to his family. He loved and cared for them and did his best to give them a good life. They lived in a small and beautiful house.

A neighbor of John was very intrigued by one habit of his. Every evening, when John came back from work, he would hang something on the tree outside his house and pick it up on his way to work next morning.

One day, the neighbor waited for John to come and asked him what was it that he hanged on the tree every day. And John said, "Workdays are filled with many challenges, problems, and concerns. All days are not the same. Some days really suck. But I do not want to carry my work

---

[17] I have focused more on family and God, as these are the most neglected and more important. But every component of HFS needs to be balanced within it. In health, diet, exercise, and positive thoughts are all important. Within diet, there has to be a balance in raw and cooked food, carbs and proteins, etc.

problems to my family. So while entering the house, I hang all the problems on the branch of this tree and ask God to take care of them during the night. And when I come out the next day, most of them are already taken care of!" Hats off to John for an amazing work-family-faith balance!

A few months back, I was so happy when I came across the Grant Study done by Harvard. It validated the point of view that I have held for decades! I heard a TEDx talk of Robert Waldinger, who was at that time the fourth director of this mammoth study! This study had been going on for more than eighty years! Seven hundred twenty-four persons from various walks of life were tracked all their lives! It started with a study of two hundred sixty-eight physically and mentally healthy Harvard college sophomores from the classes of 1939–1944.[18] It has run in tandem with a study called the Glueck Study, which included a second batch of four hundred fifty-six disadvantaged nondelinquent inner-city youths who grew up in Boston neighborhoods

---

[18] Incidentally, John F. Kennedy was one of these 268 sophomores!

between 1940 and 1945. The subjects were all male and of American nationality. The men were evaluated at least every two years by questionnaires, by information from their physicians, and in many cases, by personal interviews. Information was gathered about their mental and physical health, career enjoyment, retirement experience, and marital quality. The goal of the study was to identify predictors of healthy aging. The key finding of the study, said Robert Waldinger, was this:

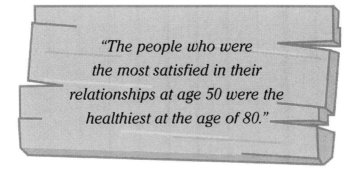

"The people who were the most satisfied in their relationships at age 50 were the healthiest at the age of 80."

The happiest and the ones who lived longest were not the rich and the famous but those who were friendly and loving and caring! It is so very obvious that beyond a certain level of income or wealth, more money or position cannot add to our happiness.

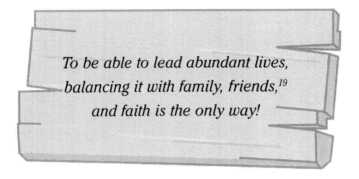

To be able to lead abundant lives, balancing it with family, friends,[19] and faith is the only way!

Once you begin your search for spiritual wisdom, something beautiful begins to happen. You see it everywhere: through others, through nature, in your thoughts, and in the beautiful silence where everything becomes clear. Keep going! Most beautiful things are waiting to be discovered.

Foundation

But however strong and well made the pillars, if the foundation is not strong, the house will collapse sooner than later. For me, God/faith is not only a component of bringing balance

---

[19] One word of caution: Social networking is part of life today and is important, but friends and family are whom you talk to and meet now and then. Two to three close friends whom you can depend on are better than a thousand FB likes!

into our lives but is also the very foundation of an abundant life! The foundation of our House of Abundance has to be love/God!

"Therefore everyone who hears these words of mine and puts them into practice is like a wise man who built his house on the rock. The rain came down, the streams rose, and the winds blew and beat against that house; yet it did not fall, because it had its foundation on the rock. But everyone who hears these words of mine and does not put them into practice is like a foolish man who built his house on sand. The rain came down, the streams rose, and the winds blew and beat against that house, and it fell with a great crash."[20]

This is exactly what had happened in the 2008 financial meltdown and COVID-19! The houses of people, who did not have faith, came down with a crash! The faith I am talking about is not a blind faith but is more like the intuitive faith and trust of a child.

---

[20]   Mathew 7:24-27 New International Version

When a child is walking holding a parent's hand, he has no worry in the world! The world may be crashing or breaking all around, but the child walks on happily, for he has intuitive trust and faith in his parents! We need to develop that kind of faith! We need to trust our Creator much more. God is our father, mother, and best friend! Heavenly Father, Divine Mother, Nature, or pure Consciousness and Spirit and Energy—whatever works for you!

I know this kind of faith cannot be developed overnight. It takes work. If we look at the two big challenges of recent years that I have been talking about—2008 financial meltdown and COVID-19 (and such challenges would keep coming in the years to come too)—we will see that the worst part of both of these was the collective fear psychosis that they created.

Our environment has a very strong influence on us unless we make a conscious effort to insulate ourselves from it.

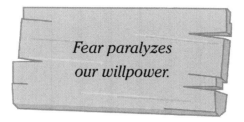

*Fear paralyzes
our willpower.*

All of us have heard the phrase "Paralyzed with fear!" That is what fear does—it paralyses our willpower. The only way to overcome this fear is by developing faith. Faith and fear cannot coexist!

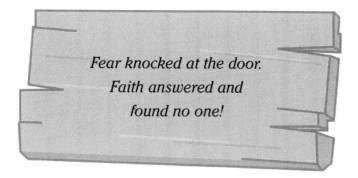

*Fear knocked at the door.
Faith answered and
found no one!*

Faith gives us courage to face life. When our will is not paralyzed, we can take rational action.

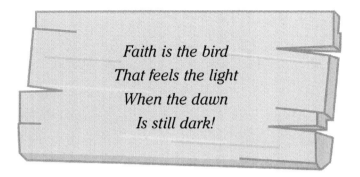

Faith is the bird
That feels the light
When the dawn
Is still dark!

During my travels around the world, I have observed that spiritually inclined, contemplative people are relatively happier and happy people are the most successful! By spiritual, I don't mean the ritualistic religious people but those who think, those who have more faith, those who believe in kindness and compassion, and those who are loving and caring! Such people are always at peace and are relatively happier and lead more abundant lives!

I know a beautiful old lady, a very close friend's mother, whom I call auntie! I am very fond of her, and she must be in her nineties now! She was always extremely lively, while her husband was a very quiet, nice gentleman! Auntie was always well dressed and beautifully made up! By the time she came to mid eighties, she became very unhappy and was very unfulfilled. Their children were in other cities and abroad, and auntie would cry often. She would always tell me that it was so good I started to meditate and became devotional early in life. Now she wanted to but was not able to do so! I could see and feel her fear and her pain, and my heart went out to her. I prayed for her and kept encouraging her to do her best.

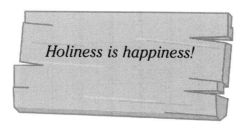

Holiness is happiness!

This need to know higher realities and to look for a meaning and purpose in life becomes stronger as we grow old. We begin to realize the futility of possessions, and we begin to question all that was once so important in our lives. But invariably, it is rather late.

God is love. God is nature. He/nature is the source of everything. Get connected and keep the connection vibrant, and all your material desires will be fulfilled too!

Millions of people think that all wealth comes from banks, factories, and jobs, and through personal ability. Yet periodic great depressions prove that there are divine laws, aside from known physical laws, that govern the physical, mental, spiritual, and material phases of life. Strive every day to be healthy, wealthy, wise, and happy, not by taking away the health, wealth, and happiness of others, but by including their happiness and welfare in your own. The happiness of individuals, of family members, and of nations depends entirely upon the law of mutual cooperation or unselfishness, and on living up to this motto: "Father, bless us, that we may remember Thee always. Let us not forget that all blessings flow from Thee."

—Paramahansa Yogananda

Suggested Actions

1. Draw a rough schedule for your work-life balance and fine-tune it over three to four weeks. Follow it without being fanatic about it. Success of 70–80 percent is good enough!
2. Meditate and/or pray every day for a minimum of fifteen minutes every morning and night—preferably thirty minutes. You can easily do it by reducing your time on social media![21]
3. Take a long weekend break every quarter and one long vacation every year.

---

[21] "I will be calmly active, actively calm. I will not become lazy and mentally ossified. Nor will I be overactive, able to earn money but unable to enjoy life. I will meditate regularly to maintain true balance" Paramahansa Yogananda.

Go ahead and begin to weave,
and the divine shall
provide the thread!

ABOUT THE AUTHOR

Ashok has had a very successful corporate career spanning four decades. He has been a life coach, friend, philosopher, and guide to hundreds of people—young and old from all spheres of life. He has a unique gift of presenting complexities of life in a very simple language with stories from his life and personal experiences.

TESTIMONIALS

Though he is not a blood relation, Ashok uncle has played a significant role in whole of my life. My dad expired when I was only 11, and he became the father figure for me in my growing years. Words could never tell the joy he brings to us.

Ashok uncle, by his example, taught me to love unconditionally and always stay positive. As a mentor he provided guidance and helped me overcome many challenges and grow into a better person. He is very wise and yet so humble and loving.

His affectionate involvement in my life has always helped me to develop self-confidence. Though we live so far away now, he is still a source of security for me. And his presence in my life is a gift to last all our lives.

*—***Sreeja Maggo***, Hongkong*

I have known Ashok for over a decade now and he has always been my go-to when my mind has been confused and I have needed someone to just listen. His gentle voice, his welcoming heart and the abundance of wisdom is such a gift. I have been truly blessed to know him.

—Bhakti Ullal, Consulting Technical Manager, Oracle, Mumbai

Words fall short to describe the kind of impact Ashok uncle's presence has had in my life. I have known him for five years, and I still keep learning something from him everyday.

He is someone who has shown me how one can actually live a full life. He is a perfect role model of a senior - physically fit and radiant, mentally cheerful and spiritually racing toward the divine infinite. His life example has given me hope, faith and courage. I simply admire and adore his immensely loving and caring heart. For Ashok uncle, this whole world is but one family. I will be eternally grateful to him for all that he has given me and done for me. I can't imagine my life without his loving guidance.

May God give him long and healthy life so that he can keep helping more and more people, and

especially youngsters, the way he has touched and shaped my life.

—Namita Raghav, German Language Teacher, Kochi

We met with uncle Ashok in Mumbai in 2018, and since then everything has changed in our lives. I don´t know if it is because of his loving meditating energy, or our conversations about abundance and Paramahansa Yogananda.

A year later he came to Guatemala, he sat with us at lake Flowers in Peten and made a drawing about the 4 pillars of abundance and explained to us while we waited for lunch. I remember imagining a circle and in the center God and Love together; around this four circles like a necklace 1 - Happiness, 2 - Gratitude, 3 - Giving and Serving, and 4 - Balance.

I am so thankful for that conversation. It has made our lives so much better. I still remember the energy, the calm in his words while he gave us such a loving message. The way I see abundance now has changed, and ever since situations around me too. It is a powerful message.

—Blanca Triquez Garcia, Architect,
Guatemala

I still can't believe that I met Ashokji through a blog. I had just started to explore spirituality. Every word that he wrote in his blog resonated so deeply with me and I instantly became a fan. It was a pleasure seeing him when he came to US for a visit. He was everything that he wrote about and more. He is selfless, wise, charming, full of love and a very fit 70 years old, I ever met! Since then he has always been there for me, whenever I need direction. I am so grateful to have met this gem of a person

—Jyoti Shah, Boston, USA

God sent me Ashok uncle some years back, when I was going through a very rough time in my life. He guided me with so much love and ease. The way he was making an impact in my life was so effortless.

At that time it was like spending time with uncle. But now I realize that his advice and talks have completely changed the way I think and handle my life. With Ashok uncle's help I've grown from inside. I can say this because now whatever situation comes to me, I am able to accept and respond without getting unduly perturbed or unhappy. Had I not met uncle, I don't know where and what I would be!

I am very grateful to God that he has sent such an amazing person like Ashok uncle, in my life.

—Sabrina Maharjan, Probity International,
Kathmandu

I met Ashok Uncle when I moved to a new society and was starting a music class. I was pleasantly surprised at his enthusiasm to learn new things and being passionate about, at such an old age. Well age is just a number and Ashok Uncle is forever young at heart!

He used to share his positive outlook on life every time we met. It not only inspired me to remain positive but also taught me that gratefulness and compassion can turn the worst of situations into something that can be easily dealt with.

I remember I was going through a set back when I lost my voice and Uncle was the first person to visit me to give me hope and courage. Not only that, he would message me daily with positive quotes that would inspire me to start my day on a positive note. And when I got my voice back, I got inspired by Uncle to start doing meditation, which boosted my health and my mind with so much positive energy. I felt like a different person and I surely improved a lot in my singing too. I know Uncle kept me in his prayers all through this, which really helped me to keep moving ahead.

I will be forever grateful to Ashok Uncle for inspiring me in so many ways.

—Himangi Vishwaroop, Singer,
Pune

Ashok is one of the few persons I really admire because he has a calm and pleasing nature even in tough project situations. He is a soul who is wise, warm, kind hearted, content with life, *overflowing with love for others and thus always giving in nature. I am sure his words of wisdom and life experiences would help us all in leading more successful and stress-free lives.*

—Harsh Tibarewala, Director TCS,
Singapore

I had the beautiful fortune of meeting Ashok at a mutual friends wedding in New Delhi several years ago. We have stayed in touch since then and his frequent correspondence has been supportive and illuminating over the years. He has given me lots of proverbs and sage advice that I find priceless. Somehow he always manages to send them at the perfect time. I find myself passing his insights along to friends and loved ones so that they can experience his brilliant wisdom as well.

—Lauren Williams, Model and Fitness Trainer,
Vancouver, Canada

If you are low, agitated, or angry - in short unhappy, all you need to do is to talk to Wahi uncle. He will give you some tip to deal with the emotion. Because as he says it is not the problem that is causing all the unhappiness, it is the response to the problem. Thank you uncle for always being there when I need help and guidance.

—Sangeeta Raghu-Punnadi, Principal
Technical Writer, Red Hat, Pune

I have known Mr. Ashok Wahi, for more than 30 years. He is a friend, brother, guide and guru. I always seek knowledge and wisdom from him and he takes so much effort to make me understand life from different perspectives!

There is so much to tell about his wisdom and unconditional love, but to tell it in one word, he is my first guru. His off and on visits and messages are so inspiring, and they motivate me to keep going even in the most challenging situations of life.

He is an inspiration to all of us, and is the wisest and the most caring person I have ever come across.

—Sakshi Narang, Yoga Teacher,
Delhi

I have known Mr. Ashok Wahi (Pa) for more than 4 years now. I have learnt so many things from him over these years; about health, spirituality, food, happiness and the list goes on! Actually, Pa is like a Potli baba to me, full of wisdom and rich experience which he keeps sharing with everyone. He is amazingly charismatic and carries a vibrant aura around him all the time.

I always consider it my blessing to be in his company and just listen and listen and listen to his words of wisdom and varied experiences.

—Anita Bhat, Mumbai

I had first met Ashok uncle during a NGO event. There is a wave of happiness or inner satisfaction which one feels when one talks to him. I have told my husband a couple of times that we should try to live our life like he does! There is so much to learn from him. If I have to describe him in two words it has to be ' Selfless' and 'Loving'.

—Vidhi Shah, Wealth Manager,
HDFC, Pune

It was a lovely morning in the amazing city of Bombay in January 2018. I was traveling with a friend around India.

On that morning we went downstairs to have breakfast at the hotel restaurant, and I saw a man, having breakfast too. He was so calm, and looked so peaceful. On that trip I was healing and searching for some answers, because of some life troubles I was going through. Suddenly, I clearly heard a voice within me, in my left ear (trust me, was very clear) the voice said to me: Talk to him! So I did! And then, like magic, all the answers came! I was like a little child again, talking and talking, with this mysterious and wise man, his name Ashok.

On that morning God gave us an extraordinary gift - uncle Ashok's friendship! That is lasting until now. He is a friend, uncle, and guide! He was the door that I needed at that time.

When I look back, there was meant to be on that morning this special and divine friendship. My healing and spiritual journey started very far away from home. I thank God for this meeting with uncle Ashok, it was like fresh air to my soul on that morning!

—Claudia Pezzaross de León,
Architect, Guatemala

I have known Ashokji and his late wife Anita, for over forty years now. In my mind and heart I have seen a great transformation in Ashok to becoming Ashokji - whom we regard as our mentor and guide now!

We are blessed to have known Ashokji so closely and his sheer presence in our lives has truly impacted and greatly inspired us in so many ways. Discussions with him on any issue relating to any matter under the sun, has always given us a very balanced, logical, rational, and all-inclusive perspective, for the highest good of all. He has enriched our lives with the example of his life of loving all and selfless service.

Ashokji has always been an avid traveller and reader and now it is a matter of great pride for us that he has penned down his personal experiences, spiritual insights and learning into this book - "4 Pillars of Abundant Life" for all of us. I am sure this book will greatly help readers lead rich, more fulfilling and happier lives. I wish and pray that he will keep guiding us by spreading love, peace and light as always!

— Sanjay Sharma, Ex MD,
Glam India Pvt Ltd, Mumbai

Ashok Wahi has been a guide to me for over 15 years. The distance doesn't matter, because we are always connected, in spirit and thoughts. I wonder - how is it that ever so often his message will impact my life? I wonder - how is it that at every turning point, his calm personality just sends me a nudge in the right direction? We come across certain people in life, because they are bearing pertinent messages for us.

—Seema Sawhney Sharma,
Sunshine Productions, Mumbai